How Do Video Game Graphics Work? The Technology Behind Mind-Blowing Games

Exploring GPUs, Ray Tracing, DLSS, and the Science of Gaming

Owen Delaney

Copyright

Disclaimer

This book is a work of nonfiction. Every effort has been made to ensure the accuracy and reliability of the information presented. However, the author and publisher make no representations or warranties regarding the completeness, accuracy, or applicability of the contents. The information is provided on an "as is" basis and should not be considered professional, legal, medical, financial, or technical advice. The reader assumes full responsibility for any decisions or actions taken based on the information in this book. The author and publisher shall not be liable for any direct, indirect, incidental, consequential, or special damages resulting from the use or reliance on the information contained herein. Any similarities to real people, organizations, or events are purely coincidental unless explicitly stated.
All trademarks, registered trademarks, and product names mentioned in this book are the property of their respective owners. Their inclusion does not imply endorsement or affiliation

Table Of Contents

Introduction

Video games have come a long way from the simple pixelated sprites of the 1970s to today's breathtakingly realistic worlds. The moment you step into a game, whether it's exploring vast open landscapes, engaging in high-speed chases, or walking through rain-soaked city streets that look almost indistinguishable from real life, you're witnessing a technological marvel at work.

But have you ever stopped to wonder—how do these stunning graphics actually come to life?

What you see on the screen isn't just a series of images; it's an intricate ballet of technology, mathematics, and creativity working seamlessly behind the scenes. Your computer or gaming console is performing billions of calculations per second to transform raw data into immersive visuals. Every shadow, every reflection in a puddle, and every explosion bursting across your screen is the result of years of innovation in

GPU architecture, rendering techniques, and AI-driven enhancements.

This book takes you on an electrifying journey into the hidden science of video game graphics—an industry that merges art, technology, and engineering to create experiences that leave us in awe. From the birth of simple 8-bit graphics to the era of Ray Tracing, DLSS, and real-time photorealism, we'll break down the core principles of how games generate visuals that push the boundaries of reality.

It's hard to believe that just a few decades ago, video games were nothing more than blocks of color moving across a screen. Take a moment to picture Pong, one of the first video games ever created. It featured two white paddles and a bouncing dot, yet at the time, it was revolutionary. Fast-forward to today, and we have games so detailed that individual pores on a character's skin, the way light refracts through water, and the movement of fabric in the wind look almost identical to real life.

The leap from simple 2D sprites to hyper-realistic 3D worlds didn't happen overnight. It was driven by technological advancements, faster GPUs, better rendering techniques, and an industry-wide obsession with pushing boundaries. Each gaming generation brought something new—3D models, texture mapping, dynamic lighting, and AI-driven physics engines—all contributing to the breathtaking visuals we now take for granted.

But what makes modern graphics so mind-blowingly realistic? Why do games today feel so immersive? And most importantly—how does your gaming device take raw data and turn it into cinematic-quality visuals?

The answer lies deep within the graphics pipeline, a behind-the-scenes process that works like magic, rendering every frame with precision.

You might be thinking—why should I care about how video game graphics work? After all, you don't need to be a car mechanic to enjoy driving, right? But here's the thing: the more you understand about what's happening under the hood, the more you appreciate the artistry and technical genius that goes into every gaming experience.

Imagine playing your favorite open-world game. The sun rises in the distance, casting golden rays through the trees. Shadows stretch realistically across the landscape, water ripples with natural fluidity, and characters move with lifelike animations. You might think, "Wow, this looks incredible!"—but what you're really seeing is a complex dance of pixels, physics, and programming working in perfect harmony.

Understanding game graphics allows you to appreciate the sheer complexity behind what you're seeing. Every lighting effect, every texture, and every particle explosion is the result of years of research and innovation. It also helps you make informed choices when buying gaming hardware, knowing how GPUs, frame rates, and resolution impact your experience.

Better understanding game performance issues can also help you diagnose why your game lags when you turn settings to ultra-high. Graphics rendering is a balancing act between performance and visual fidelity.

If you've ever dreamed of working in game development, diving into the science of game graphics is a great starting point.

To truly appreciate the magic of modern game graphics, we need to take a peek behind the curtain at the powerful technologies working tirelessly in the background.

At the heart of every stunning visual you see in a game lies the GPU (Graphics Processing Unit)—a high-performance powerhouse designed to process complex graphics calculations at lightning speed. Unlike your computer's CPU, which handles general tasks, the GPU is dedicated to rendering images, processing visual effects, and ensuring that every frame looks as stunning as possible.

But raw GPU power isn't the only thing responsible for mind-blowing game visuals. Over the years, developers have refined a variety of groundbreaking techniques to simulate real-world environments with astonishing realism.

Ray Tracing is one of the most exciting advancements in game graphics. It simulates the way light behaves in the real world, creating ultra-realistic lighting, reflections, and shadows. This technique traces the path of light in real time, making in-game environments look more natural than ever before.

DLSS (Deep Learning Super Sampling) is another revolutionary innovation. This AI-powered upscaling technology allows games to run at high resolutions without sacrificing frame rates. Thanks to machine learning, your games can now look sharper and run smoother at the same time.

Shader technology plays a crucial role in defining how objects and surfaces interact with light. From the way water shimmers to the way skin appears translucent under sunlight, shaders control the fine details that make graphics feel lifelike.

Texture mapping and normal maps bring depth and realism to in-game surfaces. Without textures, a 3D model would look like a dull, flat object. Advanced mapping techniques add detail, making everything from rough stone walls to silky fabrics look convincingly real.

Advanced physics engines ensure that game environments react naturally to movement and interaction. Whether it's the way fire spreads, how water moves, or how characters' clothing ripples in the wind, physics engines create immersive, believable experiences.

The synergy between hardware advancements and software innovations has paved the way for some of the most visually stunning games in history. But what's truly exciting is that we're only scratching the surface—the future of game graphics is set to evolve even further, bringing us even closer to the dream of fully immersive virtual worlds.

In the pages ahead, we'll take a deep dive into the core principles of video game graphics—from the fundamental building blocks of rendering to the cutting-edge advancements that are reshaping the industry.

The graphics pipeline will be explored in detail, revealing how your gaming device transforms raw data into breathtaking visuals in real time. The science behind Ray Tracing will be broken down, showing how realistic lighting and reflections are achieved. The role of AI-powered enhancements like DLSS will be examined, uncovering how modern games achieve both high performance and stunning visuals.

The importance of textures, shaders, and lighting effects will be discussed, showing how developers bring depth and realism to every game environment. Techniques for optimizing graphics performance will be explored, explaining why frame rates matter and how to find the perfect balance between visuals and speed.

The future of video game graphics will be examined, with a look at upcoming innovations, from AI-powered rendering to the rise of photorealistic graphics.

This isn't just a technical deep dive—it's a fascinating journey into the very heart of gaming visuals. Whether you're a casual gamer, a tech enthusiast, or someone who dreams of working in game development, this book will give you a newfound appreciation for the technology shaping the future of gaming.

So, buckle up—because we're about to embark on an eye-opening adventure into the science, artistry, and sheer brilliance behind video game graphics.

Get ready to see video games in a whole new light.

Chapter 1

The Basics of Video Game Graphics

Video game graphics have evolved into something truly spectacular. From simple pixelated characters bouncing across a screen to vast open-world landscapes filled with intricate details, the journey of visual storytelling in gaming has been nothing short of extraordinary. But behind the seamless motion and lifelike imagery lies a highly complex system at work—one that transforms raw data into mesmerizing visuals at lightning speed.

To truly understand how games achieve such realism, it's essential to explore the fundamental building blocks that bring them to life. This chapter takes a deep dive into the core principles of video game graphics, unraveling the intricate process of how a game goes from mere code to an immersive visual experience.

At the heart of it all is the Graphics Processing Unit (GPU)—the powerhouse responsible for rendering images in real time. By performing millions of calculations per second, the GPU turns raw instructions into the vibrant, detailed visuals that define modern gaming. But the GPU alone isn't enough; other crucial elements like pixels, polygons, shaders, and lighting effects play an equally significant role.

For a game to appear smooth and immersive, each frame must be rendered with precision and efficiency. Every frame is a work of art, carefully crafted by blending multiple layers of textures, colors, and visual effects—all calculated in fractions of a second.

How Video Games Display Images on a Screen

When you boot up your favorite game, the images that appear on your screen are not static pictures but rather a series of rapidly changing frames. These frames, when displayed in quick succession, create the illusion of motion—much like a flipbook animation.

At its core, a video game is simply a program that sends a continuous stream of instructions to the computer's hardware. The game engine, acting as the brain of the operation, determines what needs to be displayed and how it should look based on the player's input, physics calculations, and environmental interactions.

The display output in modern games operates on the principle of real-time rendering. Unlike pre-rendered animations seen in movies, where every frame is carefully crafted beforehand, video games must generate each frame dynamically based on constantly changing conditions. Whether it's an explosion, a character jumping, or a shadow shifting in the wind, every detail is processed and displayed in real time.

Each image on the screen is composed of pixels—tiny colored squares that blend to form a complete picture. A typical gaming monitor or TV screen contains millions of these pixels, each capable of displaying a range of colors. The GPU determines the color and brightness of each pixel by processing multiple layers of graphical data, ensuring that every frame appears smooth and visually accurate.

But displaying an image isn't just about placing colors on a screen. It involves calculating how light interacts with surfaces, how objects cast shadows, and how movement affects perception—all of which require an immense amount of processing power.

As games grow more sophisticated, the demand for higher resolution, faster frame rates, and improved visual effects continues to push the boundaries of what's possible. To keep up with these demands, modern GPUs employ advanced rendering techniques to generate lifelike graphics at unprecedented speeds.

The Role of GPUs (Graphics Processing Units)

At the center of every visually stunning game is the Graphics Processing Unit (GPU)—a dedicated piece of hardware designed to handle the heavy lifting of rendering images. Unlike a computer's Central Processing Unit (CPU), which focuses on general tasks like running applications and managing system operations, the GPU is specialized for graphics-related computations.

The reason GPUs are so effective at rendering video game graphics is their ability to process thousands of tasks simultaneously. Whereas a CPU operates sequentially—handling one task at a time—the GPU contains hundreds or even thousands of cores that work in parallel to perform massive calculations all at once.

When a game is running, the GPU is responsible for determining where every object should be positioned, how lighting should interact with surfaces, and how textures should be mapped onto 3D models. It does this by breaking down complex scenes into smaller components, known as polygons, and applying shading techniques to simulate depth, texture, and realism.

Another critical aspect of GPU performance is frame rate, measured in frames per second (FPS). The higher the FPS, the smoother the game appears. Most modern games aim for at least 60 FPS, while high-performance systems can push beyond 120 FPS for ultra-smooth gameplay.

One of the most significant advancements in GPU technology is Ray Tracing, a technique that accurately simulates how light behaves in the real world. By tracing the path of light rays and calculating their interactions with surfaces, Ray Tracing creates breathtakingly realistic reflections, shadows, and ambient lighting effects. While this technology was once reserved for high-budget CGI in movies, modern GPUs have made it accessible for real-time gaming.

The evolution of GPUs has not only enhanced graphical fidelity but also introduced groundbreaking features like AI-driven upscaling (DLSS), which uses machine learning to boost performance without sacrificing image quality. These advancements have transformed gaming into a visually immersive experience that was once thought impossible.

Pixels, Polygons, and Shaders: The Building Blocks of Game Visuals

Every visual element in a video game—whether it's a character, a tree, or an explosion—is composed of fundamental components that work together to create a cohesive image. The three main building blocks of game graphics are pixels, polygons, and shaders.

Pixels are the foundation of every digital image. Each screen is made up of millions of these tiny squares, and their arrangement determines the clarity and sharpness of the image. Higher resolutions, such as 4K, contain more pixels, resulting in sharper and more detailed visuals.

Polygons are the building blocks of 3D models. Every object in a game world is made up of thousands (or even millions) of polygons that form its shape. The more polygons an object has, the smoother and more detailed it appears. Early 3D games relied on low-polygon models with jagged edges, but modern titles utilize high-polygon counts for near-photorealistic quality.

Shaders add depth and realism to objects by controlling how light interacts with surfaces. These small programs run on the GPU and determine an object's color, texture, transparency, and reflectivity. Advanced shaders can simulate complex effects like water ripples, fire embers, and even realistic skin textures.

Together, these three elements work in harmony to construct the breathtaking visuals seen in today's games. By optimizing their use, developers can create incredibly immersive experiences that push the limits of visual storytelling.

The Frame-by-Frame Rendering Process

The process of rendering a video game scene is a complex, multi-step operation that takes place within milliseconds. Each frame is built layer by layer, with every detail carefully calculated to maintain smooth performance and visual accuracy.

Rendering begins with the geometry stage, where the game engine determines the position and shape of all objects in the scene. Next comes the lighting stage, where the system calculates how light sources interact with objects, casting shadows and reflections.

Once lighting is applied, textures and shaders are layered onto the objects, adding depth, color, and realism. The GPU then processes post-processing effects like motion blur, depth of field, and bloom lighting to enhance the cinematic feel of the scene.

Finally, the completed frame is sent to the display at lightning speed. This entire process repeats dozens of times per second, creating the illusion of continuous movement.

With the relentless pursuit of innovation, the rendering process continues to evolve, pushing video game graphics closer to the realm of reality.

Chapter 2

The Graphics Pipeline – Turning Data into Stunning Visuals

Video games are a marvel of modern technology, blending art, physics, and real-time computation into immersive digital worlds. But beneath the stunning visuals lies an intricate system designed to process and render images at incredible speeds. This system, known as the graphics pipeline, is the backbone of video game graphics, transforming raw data into breathtaking visuals in real-time.

The graphics pipeline is a carefully orchestrated sequence of steps that ensures every element in a game scene—from characters and landscapes to lighting and reflections—appears exactly as intended. It determines how objects are drawn, how light interacts with surfaces, and how efficiently a game can run without sacrificing quality.

Understanding the graphics pipeline is key to appreciating the technology that makes modern gaming possible. Whether you're admiring the intricate details of a character's armor or the realistic reflections on a rain-soaked street, every pixel on the screen has undergone an elaborate transformation behind the scenes.

Understanding the Rendering Pipeline

At its core, the rendering pipeline is the process by which a computer converts 3D models into 2D images that can be displayed on a screen. This transformation is far more complex than simply drawing objects on a canvas; it involves mathematical calculations, physics simulations, and lighting effects, all executed in real-time.

The pipeline is divided into several key stages, each playing a critical role in rendering the final image. Every object in a game starts as raw 3D data, which the GPU processes through a series of transformations before turning it into the final imagedisplayed on the screen. These transformations ensure that objects maintain proper shape, depth, and realism, even when the player moves the camera or interacts with the environment. The pipeline handles everything from positioning objects in a 3D space to applyingtextures, lighting, and shading effects that make the game world look realistic. Every object in a scene, whether it's a towering skyscraper or a tiny pebble, must go through this pipeline to be accurately represented on the screen.

The process is designed to be incredibly fast and efficient, as games need to render dozens of frames per second to create smooth motion. To achieve this, the graphics pipeline relies on a series of specialized stages, each responsible for a specific aspect of rendering. These stages work in harmony to ensure that visuals remain high-quality while maintaining optimal performance.

Stages of the Graphics Pipeline

The graphics pipeline consists of several key stages, each performing a specific function to transform raw data into a final image. These stages—vertex processing, geometry processing, rasterization, shading, and display—work in sequence, ensuring that every frame appears detailed and realistic.

Vertex Processing

Every 3D object in a video game is made up of points called vertices, which define its shape and structure. A single vertex stores information about its position in 3D space, its color, texture coordinates, and even how it reacts to lighting. During vertex processing, the GPU takes this raw vertex data and transforms it so that it fits correctly into the game world.

This transformation involves several key steps. The GPU first adjusts the position of each vertex according to the game's camera, ensuring that objects appear from the correct perspective. Next, it applies any animations or deformations, such as the movement of a character's limbs or the bending of grass in the wind.

Once all necessary transformations are complete, the processed vertices move to the next stage of the pipeline, where the game world begins to take shape.

Geometry Processing

After vertex processing, the GPU begins forming the basic structure of objects by connecting vertices to create polygons, usually triangles. This is because triangles are the simplest shape that can be used to construct complex 3D models.

In this stage, the GPU also performs a crucial optimization step called culling. Culling removes any polygons that won't be visible to the player, such as the backside of an object or anything hidden behind another structure. By eliminating unnecessary calculations, culling improves performance and allows the GPU to focus on rendering only what the player can see.

Another key technique used in geometry processing is **tess
ellation**, a process that dynamically increases the number of polygons in a model to enhance visual detail. Instead of manually creating highly detailed models with millions

of polygons, tessellation allows the GPU to generate extra geometry only when needed.

For example, a rocky surface that appears smooth from a distance can become more detailed and rugged as the player approaches. This dynamic adjustment helps create more immersive and realistic environments without overloading the GPU with unnecessary detail. By using tessellation, game developers can strike a perfect balance between visual quality and performance, allowing players to experience highly detailed worlds that adapt seamlessly to their movements.

A similar technique, known as adaptive tessellation, takes this concept a step further by adjusting the level of detail based on the player's viewpoint and distance. Objects closer to the camera receive more tessellation, while distant objects use fewer polygons, conserving processing power. This approach ensures that performance remains smooth, even in expansive, open-world games where countless objects populate the environment.

Through these optimizations, the geometry processing stage not only constructs the physical structure of the game world but also ensures it does so with maximum efficiency, setting the stage for the visual enhancements that follow in the rendering process.

How GPUs Optimize Speed and Efficiency

Modern video games demand immense processing power to generate lifelike graphics at high frame rates. To achieve this, Graphics Processing Units (GPUs) are designed with specialized architecture that prioritizes speed, efficiency, and parallel processing. Unlike CPUs, which handle a broad range of tasks sequentially, GPUs excel at processing thousands of operations simultaneously, making them ideal for rendering complex visuals in real time.

One of the most significant ways GPUs optimize performance is through parallel processing. Instead of handling one calculation at a time, GPUs contain thousands of small cores that work together to process multiple calculations simultaneously. This ability allows GPUs to quickly transform large amounts of raw data into detailed images at speeds of 60 frames per second (FPS) or higher.

Another crucial optimization technique is tile-based rendering, used by many modern GPUs. Instead of rendering an entire scene at once, the GPU breaks the screen into smaller sections called tiles, processes them separately, and then combines them to form the final image. This method significantly reduces memory bandwidth usage, preventing bottlenecks and improving rendering efficiency.

To further enhance speed, GPUs use caching mechanisms that store frequently accessed data in fast memory locations. This reduces the need to repeatedly fetch data from slower memory, improving rendering performance. Techniques like level-of-detail (LOD) scaling also optimize speed by reducing the complexity of objects that are far from the player's viewpoint. Instead of rendering every distant tree or building in full detail, LOD dynamically lowers the polygon count, saving processing power without affecting visual fidelity.

Another powerful optimization technique is asynchronous compute, which allows different GPU tasks—such as rendering, physics calculations, and AI processing—to run simultaneously rather than waiting for one another to finish. This approach maximizes GPU utilization, ensuring smoother gameplay and more stable frame rates, especially in graphically intense scenes.

Additionally, modern GPUs leverage upscaling technologies like Deep Learning Super Sampling (DLSS) and FidelityFX Super Resolution (FSR). These AI-driven techniques allow games to render at lower resolutions while using machine learning to intelligently upscale the image, delivering near-native quality visuals at a fraction of the processing cost. This technology significantly enhances performance, making high-resolution gaming accessible even on less powerful hardware.

By combining these techniques, GPUs achieve a balance between stunning graphics and real-time performance, enabling modern games to run smoothly while maintaining visual excellence.

Chapter 3

The Power of GPUs and Graphics Cards

Video game graphics have come a long way, evolving from pixelated sprites to stunning, photorealistic visuals that immerse players in vast digital worlds. At the heart of this transformation is the Graphics Processing Unit (GPU)—a specialized piece of hardware designed to handle the intense graphical computations required for modern gaming. While the Central Processing Unit (CPU) is often considered the brain of a computer, the GPU is its artistic soul, responsible for rendering everything players see on their screens.

Over the years, GPUs have undergone a massive evolution, growing more powerful with each generation. Today, they are not just essential for gaming but also for applications in artificial intelligence, video editing, and scientific computing. But what makes a GPU so different from a CPU? How have graphics cards evolved to become the high-performance powerhouses they are today? And what exactly happens inside a GPU to create the seamless and visually stunning gaming experiences we enjoy?

To understand the full power of GPUs and graphics cards, let's break down their functions, evolution, and internal workings to see how they shape the future of gaming.

What Makes GPUs Different from CPUs?

At first glance, CPUs and GPUs might seem similar—they are both processors designed to execute computations and process data. However, their core differences lie in how they handle tasks.

A CPU (Central Processing Unit) is designed for serial processing, meaning it excels at executing tasks one at a time in a fast and organized manner. It is responsible for general system operations, such as running the operating system, managing input and output devices, and executing complex calculations. CPUs typically have a small number of high-performance cores (usually between 4 and 16 in modern processors), optimized for handling a wide variety of tasks efficiently.

A GPU (Graphics Processing Unit), on the other hand, is designed for parallel processing—the ability to handle thousands of smaller tasks simultaneously. This makes it incredibly well-suited for rendering graphics, where millions of pixels need to be processed in real time. Instead of a few powerful cores like a CPU, a GPU features hundreds or even thousands of smaller, specialized cores, allowing it to process massive amounts of data at once.

This difference is why CPUs are great for general computing tasks, while GPUs dominate when it comes to graphics rendering, AI processing, and high-performance computing. In gaming, this means that while the CPU handles tasks like physics calculations, AI behavior, and game logic, the GPU takes care of everything visual—textures, lighting, shadows, reflections, and effects.

GPUs also use shader cores, which specialize in rendering techniques such as shading, anti-aliasing, and ray tracing. This allows them to produce visually stunning environments, realistic character animations, and fluid motion—all at high frame rates.

The Evolution of GPUs from Early Gaming to Today

The history of GPUs is a story of rapid technological advancement, driven by the demand for better graphics, faster rendering, and more immersive gaming experiences.

Early Gaming and 2D Graphics
In the early days of video games, graphics were handled entirely by the CPU, which could only process simple 2D images and sprites. Games like Pong (1972) and Space Invaders (1978) used frame buffers to store pixel data, and graphical elements were rendered using basic techniques.

As games became more complex, dedicated graphics chips were introduced to offload some of the visual processing from the CPU. These early chips could manipulate sprites and backgrounds but lacked the computational power for true 3D rendering.

The Rise of 3D Graphics and the First GPUs

The 1990s marked the beginning of 3D gaming, with titles like Doom (1993) and Quake (1996) pushing the boundaries of real-time graphics. To support these advancements, companies like NVIDIA, ATI (now AMD), and 3dfx developed the first dedicated GPUs, which introduced hardware acceleration for 3D rendering.

In 1999, NVIDIA released the GeForce 256, the first GPU capable of hardware transform and lighting (T&L), a major leap forward in rendering technology. This allowed 3D models to be processed directly on the graphics card, reducing the load on the CPU and enabling smoother, more realistic graphics.

Modern GPUs and Ray Tracing Revolution

Fast forward to today, and GPUs have become incredibly powerful, capable of rendering cinematic-quality visuals in real-time. Technologies like ray tracing, AI-driven upscaling (DLSS), and real-time global illumination have transformed gaming, making virtual worlds more immersive than ever.

The latest GPUs from NVIDIA (GeForce RTX series), AMD (Radeon RX series), and Intel (Arc GPUs) feature dedicated ray tracing cores, machine learning capabilities, and high-speed memory to handle .

Graphics cards are the driving force behind gaming visuals, enabling stunning environments, realistic animations, and high frame rates. As technology advances, GPUs continue to push the limits of what's possible, bringing us closer to lifelike digital worlds. The power of modern GPUs is not just shaping games—it's revolutionizing industries, from AI research to film production, and beyond.

The Difference Between Real-Time and Pre-Rendered Graphics

Video game graphics fall into two main categories: real-time rendering and pre-rendered graphics. Both serve distinct purposes, but the difference lies in how and when the images are generated.

Real-time rendering occurs on-the-fly as the game is being played. Every frame is generated in a fraction of a second, adapting dynamically to player inputs and environmental changes. This type of rendering is essential for interactive experiences, such as open-world games, virtual reality (VR), and competitive multiplayer titles. Because every frame must be processed instantly, real-time rendering requires extreme efficiency, forcing developers to make trade-offs between graphical fidelity and performance.

Real-time graphics rely heavily on optimizations like rasterization, shaders, and LOD scaling to ensure smooth frame rates. While modern advancements like ray tracing have brought real-time lighting and reflections closer to cinematic quality, achieving the same level of visual detail as pre-rendered graphics remains a challenge due to hardware limitations.

Pre-rendered graphics, on the other hand, are created in advance and stored as video files or pre-generated images. This approach is commonly used in cutscenes, CGI movies, and visual effects in film production. Since pre-rendered sequences do not need to be processed in real time, they can feature unlimited polygon counts, advanced lighting calculations, and complex physics simulations without worrying about frame rate performance.

While pre-rendered graphics allow for cinematic-quality visuals, they come with limitations. Unlike real-time rendering, they lack interactivity—players cannot influence lighting, camera angles, or object placement in pre-rendered scenes. Additionally, pre-rendered assets consume significantly more storage space, as every frame is pre-generated rather than dynamically calculated.

Some games blend both approaches to enhance storytelling and immersion. For example, a game may use pre-rendered cutscenes for dramatic storytelling moments while relying on real-time graphics for seamless gameplay transitions. This hybrid approach ensures that games maintain visual consistency while allowing for engaging, interactive experiences.

As hardware technology advances, the line between real-time and pre-rendered graphics continues toblur. With powerful GPUs, advanced rendering techniques, and AI-driven upscaling, real-time graphics are reaching cinematic levels, making modern games more visually stunning than ever.

The gaming industry continues to push the boundaries of real-time rendering, incorporating techniques such as real-time ray tracing, global illumination, and AI-enhanced textures to bring unparalleled realism to interactive experiences. As a result, the gap between real-time and pre-rendered graphics is narrowing, offering players breathtaking visuals without sacrificing performance.

With future advancements in hardware acceleration, cloud computing, and machine learning, real-time rendering will likely surpass traditional pre-rendered graphics in both quality and efficiency. The ability to generate photorealistic visuals on-the-fly is no longer just a goal—it's becoming a reality, reshaping how games are developed and experienced.

Chapter 4

Ray Tracing – The Key to Realistic Lighting

Video game graphics have evolved dramatically over the decades, transforming from simple pixelated visuals to hyper-realistic environments that rival the real world. Among the many advancements that have shaped modern gaming, ray tracing stands out as a groundbreaking innovation. This technology revolutionizes the way light interacts with objects in a virtual world, bringing an unprecedented level of realism to reflections, shadows, and global illumination.

For decades, game developers relied on traditional rendering techniques like rasterization, which approximated lighting effects using pre-baked shadows and screen-space reflections. While these methods were efficient, they often resulted in unrealistic lighting behavior, where shadows looked too sharp or reflections seemed inaccurate. Ray tracing changes this entirely by simulating the way light travels in real life, allowing for lifelike visuals that enhance immersion in gaming experiences.

The shift toward ray tracing didn't happen overnight. While Hollywood films have used ray tracing for years to render CGI effects, the technology was far too computationally expensive for real-time gaming. It wasn't until the introduction of NVIDIA RTX graphics cards in 2018 that real-time ray tracing became a reality. With powerful hardware acceleration, modern GPUs now have the ability to trace individual rays of light, calculate their interactions, and generate dynamic lighting effects in real-time.

Ray tracing is particularly transformative in games that rely on atmosphere and visual fidelity. Titles like Cyberpunk 2077, Minecraft RTX, and Control showcase how accurately simulated light can create stunning environments, making reflections appear on water surfaces, shadows soften naturally, and light bounce off objects in a way that mimics reality. However, this level of realism comes at a cost—ray tracing is computationally intensive and requires cutting-edge hardware to run smoothly.

Despite its demands, ray tracing is rapidly becoming a standard in next-gen gaming. Console manufacturers like Sony and Microsoft have integrated hardware-accelerated ray tracing into the PlayStation 5 and Xbox Series X, signaling a shift toward more realistic graphics across the industry. As technology advances, ray tracing will continue to push the boundaries of visual fidelity, making games look more cinematic and immersive than ever before.

What is Ray Tracing?

Ray tracing is a rendering technique that simulates the natural behavior of light by tracing the path of individual rays as they travel through a scene. Unlike traditional rasterization, which relies on tricks and approximations to create lighting effects, ray tracing calculates how light interacts with surfaces, producing highly realistic reflections, refractions, and shadows.

At its core, ray tracing works by simulating the way light behaves in the real world. When you look at an object, what you're actually seeing is light bouncing off its surface and entering your eyes. In a game, ray tracing replicates this process by generating rays from a virtual camera, determining how they interact with different objects, and rendering the final image based on those calculations.

One of the most significant aspects of ray tracing is its ability to create physically accurate reflections. In older games, reflections were often achieved using cube maps or screen-space reflections, which had limitations. For example, in screen-space reflections, an object could only reflect what was currently on the screen, meaning that objects outside the player's view wouldn't appear in reflections. With ray tracing, reflections are based on actual light rays, meaning they can display off-screen objects, creating a much more convincing effect.

Another crucial feature of ray tracing is dynamic shadows. In traditional rendering, shadows were often pre-baked into textures or generated using shadow maps, which could look unrealistic due to their fixed nature. Ray-traced shadows, on the other hand, change dynamically based on the position of the light source, resulting in softer and more natural -looking shadows that gradually fade, mimicking how light behaves in reality. This effect is particularly noticeable in scenes with multiple light sources or moving objects, where traditional techniques often produce unnatural, harsh edges. By using ray tracing, shadows are no longer static or overly sharp—they blend seamlessly with the environment, adding depth and realism that enhances the overall immersion.

Another significant advantage of ray tracing is ambient occlusion, which determines how exposed each point in a scene is to ambient lighting. In rasterized graphics, ambient occlusion is often simulated using screen-space techniques, which can lead to unnatural artifacts and inaccuracies. Ray-traced ambient occlusion, however, calculates these effects more precisely, ensuring that crevices, corners, and occluded areas receive realistic shading, enhancing the sense of depth.

The computational cost of ray tracing is high, which is why many games offer hybrid rendering techniques—combining ray tracing with traditional rasterization. This approach allows developers to selectively apply ray-traced effects, such as reflections or global illumination, while still using rasterized methods for other aspects of the scene. This balance helps optimize performance while delivering the visual benefits of ray tracing.

As game developers continue to refine their use of ray tracing, the technology is becoming more accessible. Game engines like Unreal Engine 5, Unity, and CryEngine have integrated ray tracing support, allowing developers to harness its power with greater efficiency. Even older games are being updated with ray-traced enhancements, breathing new life into classic titles with improved lighting and realism.

With hardware advancements and optimized software, ray tracing is on track to become a standard feature in video game graphics. The level of realism it provides is unmatched, transforming digital environments into lifelike worlds that react to light just as they do in reality. While it remains a demanding technology, ongoing improvements in GPU architecture and AI-driven denoising techniques are making real-time ray tracing more practical, paving the way for the next generation of visually stunning games.

How Light Behaves in the Real World vs. Video Games

Light is a fundamental part of how we perceive the world. In reality, light originates from various sources, such as the sun, lamps, or fire, and interacts with objects in complex ways. It can reflect, refract, scatter, and diffuse, creating natural effects like shadows, color blending, and brightness variations. Every time light hits a surface, it bounces in multiple directions, affecting nearby objects and creating subtle color shifts—a phenomenon known as global illumination.

In the real world, light behaves according to the principles of physics. When it strikes a mirror-like surface, it reflects at the same angle at which it arrived, producing clear and accurate reflections. When it passes through a transparent object, such as glass or water, it bends due to refraction, causing distortions. Additionally, light gets absorbed differently depending on a material's properties—metal reflects more, while fabric or wood absorbs and diffuses light, leading to softer and more natural illumination.

Shadows in the real world are also dynamic and complex. Their sharpness depends on the size of the light source and distance—a small, intense light like a flashlight creates crisp shadows, while a large, diffused light like an overcast sky produces soft, gradual shading. Another key aspect of real-world lighting is caustics, which are patterns created when light passes through transparent objects or reflects off curved surfaces, such as the rippling effect at the bottom of a swimming pool.

In contrast, video games have historically relied on rasterization to approximate light behavior. Rasterization is a faster but less accurate method of rendering, where lighting and shadows are often precomputed or simulated using techniques like baked lighting, shadow maps, and screen-space reflections (SSR). These methods allow games to run smoothly but come with limitations, such as reflections that only display what's visible on-screen or shadows that don't update realistically when light sources move.

Ray tracing, however, is changing this landscape by simulating the real-world behavior of light in real time. It accurately models reflections, refractions, and global illumination, making scenes appear more lifelike. Unlike rasterization, which estimates lighting effects, ray tracing calculates the actual path of light rays as they interact with objects, resulting in more realistic and immersive visuals.

This shift to ray tracing is pushing video game graphics closer to photorealism, making lighting behave more naturally and enhancing the overall gaming experience. However, due to its high computational cost, real-time ray tracing is still evolving, with optimizations like Deep Learning Super Sampling (DLSS) and FSR)** helping to balance performance and visual quality.

One of the most noticeable improvements brought by ray tracing is the accuracy of real-time reflections. Traditional screen-space reflections (SSR) could only display reflections of objects that were already rendered on the screen. This meant that if an object was outside the player's view, it wouldn't appear in a reflection. With ray tracing, reflections are calculated based on actual light rays bouncing around the scene, allowing off-screen objects to appear realistically in mirrors, water, or polished surfaces.

Global illumination is another major enhancement. In real life, light doesn't just illuminate an object and stop—it bounces off surfaces, affecting the colors and brightness of surrounding areas. Ray tracing enables games to simulate this effect dynamically, making lighting look far more natural than pre-baked solutions. A red wall, for example, will subtly cast a reddish hue onto nearby objects, just as it would in reality.

Shadows also benefit greatly from ray tracing. Ray-traced shadows adapt based on the size, intensity, and position of light sources, creating soft edges and realistic depth. Traditional methods, such as shadow maps, often produced jagged or overly sharp shadows that didn't change naturally as the light source moved. Ray tracing eliminates these inconsistencies, leading to more immersive environments.

While the improvements are significant, the biggest challenge remains performance impact. Ray tracing requires a substantial amount of computing power, as each individual ray must be traced, calculated, and rendered in real time. This is why most modern games that support ray tracing also include performance-enhancing technologies like DLSS (Deep Learning Super Sampling) from NVIDIA and FSR (FidelityFX Super Resolution) from AMD. These AI-based upscaling techniques allow games to render at a lower resolution and then intelligently upscale the image, reducing the workload while maintaining visual quality.

As hardware continues to advance, ray tracing is expected to become a standard feature in gaming. With upcoming GPU architectures improving efficiency, and game developers optimizing their engines for ray-traced effects, the technology will continue to evolve, bringing even more realistic lighting, reflections, and shadows to future .

The Role of NVIDIA RTX and AMD Radeon in Ray Tracing

Ray tracing has transformed the way video games render light, shadows, and reflections, but achieving real-time ray tracing requires immense computational power. This is where dedicated graphics hardware from NVIDIA RTX and AMD Radeon comes into play. Both companies have developed specialized GPU architectures that accelerate ray tracing, making it feasible for gaming and real-time applications.

NVIDIA RTX:

NVIDIA revolutionized real-time ray tracing with the introduction of the GeForce RTX 20-series (Turing architecture) in 2018. These GPUs were the first to include RT Cores, specialized hardware designed to handle ray-tracing calculations. By offloading the complex task of simulating light interactions to these dedicated cores, NVIDIA made real-time ray tracing a reality for gamers.

Following the initial release, NVIDIA continued to enhance ray tracing with the RTX 30-series (Ampere architecture) and RTX 40-series (Ada Lovelace architecture). Each new generation brought improvements in performance, power efficiency, and rendering capabilities. The RTX 30-series introduced second-generation RT Cores and third-generation Tensor Cores, which work in tandem to deliver smoother frame rates and higher visual quality.

One of NVIDIA's standout technologies is Deep Learning Super Sampling (DLSS). DLSS uses artificial intelligence to upscale lower-resolution images, maintaining crisp visuals while reducing the computational load on the GPU. This technology is crucial for making ray tracing accessible, as it allows gamers to experience high-quality ray-traced effects without sacrificing performance.

Key NVIDIA Ray Tracing Technologies:

RT Cores: Dedicated cores that accelerate ray-tracing computations, enabling real-time reflections, shadows, and global illumination.

Tensor Cores: Specialized cores for AI-driven tasks, including DLSS, which boosts performance in ray-traced games.

DLSS (Deep Learning Super Sampling): AI-powered upscaling that enhances visual fidelity and frame rates, making ray tracing viable even on mid-range GPUs.

NVIDIA Reflex: Reduces system latency in competitive games, enhancing responsiveness even with ray tracing enabled.

NVIDIA's RTX GPUs have set the standard for ray-tracing performance in modern gaming, with popular titles like Cyberpunk

2077, Control, Battlefield V, and Minecraft RTX showcasing the stunning visual effects made possible by RTX technology.

AMD Radeon:

AMD entered the ray-tracing arena with the Radeon RX 6000 series (RDNA 2 architecture) in 2020. Unlike NVIDIA's approach of using separate RT Cores, AMD integrated Ray Accelerators directly into its Compute Units (CUs). These Ray Accelerators are responsible for handling ray-tracing calculations, although they are less efficient than NVIDIA's dedicated hardware.

The Radeon RX 7000 series (RDNA 3 architecture) improved on this design by introducing second-generation Ray Accelerators, enhancing ray-tracing efficiency and reducing the performance gap with NVIDIA. AMD has also focused on balancing ray-tracing capabilities with traditional rasterization performance, ensuring that its GPUs offer solid performance across a wide range of games.

A significant advantage for AMD is its FidelityFX Super Resolution (FSR) technology. Unlike DLSS, which requires specialized Tensor Cores, FSR is an open-source upscaling solution that works on a broader range of hardware, including older GPUs and even NVIDIA cards. FSR helps boost frame rates in ray-traced games by rendering at a lower resolution and then upscaling the image, preserving visual quality while improving performance.

Key AMD Ray Tracing Technologies:

Ray Accelerators: Integrated into Compute Units to speed up ray-tracing calculations, providing hardware-accelerated ray tracing across AMD's GPU lineup.

FidelityFX Super Resolution (FSR): A versatile upscaling technology that improves performance in ray-traced games without requiring specialized hardware.

Infinity Cache: A high-speed cache that reduces memory latency, enhancing ray-tracing performance and overall GPU efficiency.

Radeon Super Resolution (RSR): Driver-based upscaling that applies FSR-like enhancements to any game, even those without native FSR support.

While AMD's ray-tracing performance initially lagged behind NVIDIA, ongoing improvements have made Radeon GPUs a viable choice for gamers looking to experience ray-traced visuals. Games like Far Cry 6, Resident Evil Village, and God of War (PC) showcase how AMD's hardware can deliver impressive lighting, reflections, and shadow effects.

Comparing NVIDIA RTX and AMD Radeon in Ray Tracing:

1. Performance:

NVIDIA's dedicated RT Cores generally provide better ray-tracing performance, especially in demanding titles.

AMD's integrated Ray Accelerators offer solid ray tracing but may require FSR to maintain smooth frame rates in intensive games.

2. Upscaling Technologies:

DLSS (NVIDIA) is more advanced, utilizing AI to deliver superior upscaling results with less performance loss.

FSR (AMD) is more versatile, working across a broader range of Got it! I'll ensure each chapter flows smoothly, with at least 500 words before diving into subheadings. Each subheading will have at least 1,000 words, free of plagiarism, paraphrased for originality, and optimized for Amazon KDP. I'll also keep the buyer's perspective in mind while writing. No conclusions will be added at the end.

Chapter 5

DLSS (Deep Learning Super Sampling) – AI-Enhanced Graphics

The evolution of video game graphics has always been a battle between fidelity and performance. As gaming hardware advances, players expect increasingly realistic visuals, from ray-traced reflections to ultra-high-resolution textures. However, these graphical improvements come with a significant cost—higher computational demands, which can reduce frame rates and impact overall gameplay smoothness.

For years, gamers have had to choose between visual quality and performance. Lowering resolution and graphical settings boosts frame rates but results in a less immersive experience with blurry textures and jagged edges. On the other hand, running games at high resolutions like 4K can push even the most powerful GPUs to their limits, leading to stuttering and lag.

This is where Deep Learning Super Sampling (DLSS) comes in. Developed by NVIDIA, DLSS is a revolutionary AI-powered upscaling technology designed to bridge the gap between high-quality visuals and smooth performance. Instead of relying solely on raw GPU power, DLSS leverages artificial intelligence to render frames at a lower resolution and then upscale them to a higher resolution with minimal loss in detail. The result? Games that look nearly identical to their native high-resolution counterparts but run at significantly higher frame rates.

AI-enhanced graphics have transformed gaming, allowing players to experience breathtaking visuals without compromising performance. From cinematic single-player experiences to fast-paced competitive titles,

DLSS has reshaped how modern games are rendered. With each new iteration—DLSS 1.0, 2.0, and now DLSS 3—NVIDIA continues to refine the technology, making it more efficient and visually impressive than ever.

To fully appreciate DLSS, it's essential to understand how it works, why it matters, and how it compares to alternative upscaling technologies like AMD FidelityFX Super Resolution (FSR) and traditional upscaling methods.

What is DLSS and Why Does It Matter?

Deep Learning Super Sampling (DLSS) is NVIDIA's AI-driven image upscaling technology designed to improve gaming performance while maintaining visual fidelity. Unlike traditional resolution scaling, which simply stretches an image to fit a higher resolution, DLSS employs deep learning algorithms to intelligently reconstruct details, creating an image that looks nearly as sharp as a native resolution render.

DLSS matters because it solves one of the biggest challenges in gaming: balancing performance and graphical fidelity. As modern games implement resource-intensive features like ray tracing, maintaining a stable frame rate at high resolutions has become increasingly difficult. DLSS allows players to enjoy 4K-like visuals while rendering at a lower internal resolution, significantly reducing the GPU workload.

The fundamental principle behind DLSS is that it renders a game at a lower resolution (such as 1080p or 1440p) and then uses machine learning to upscale the image to a higher resolution (1440p, 4K, or even 8K). By training on a vast dataset of high-quality images, DLSS can predict and reconstruct missing details, resulting in a final image that closely resembles native rendering.

Why DLSS is a Game-Changer

1. Higher Frame Rates Without Sacrificing Quality

Running a game at native 4K resolution requires substantial GPU power, often leading to frame rate drops.

DLSS renders at a lower resolution but upscales the image, allowing for smoother gameplay while retaining visual clarity.

2. AI-Powered Image Reconstruction

Instead of simple upscaling, DLSS uses AI-trained models to intelligently predict details, making textures and objects appear sharper than traditional upscaling techniques.

3. Ray Tracing Becomes More Accessible

Ray tracing significantly enhances lighting, shadows, and reflections but is notoriously demanding on hardware.

DLSS allows ray-traced games to run at playable frame rates without compromising graphical fidelity.

4. Reduces GPU Workload

By rendering at a lower resolution and reconstructing details with AI, DLSS helps GPUs maintain higher efficiency and lower power consumption.

5. Better Than Traditional Upscaling Methods

Unlike bilinear or bicubic upscaling, which can cause noticeable blurring and pixelation, DLSS delivers crisper, more detailed visuals.

Since its initial release, DLSS has undergone multiple upgrades. DLSS 2.0 introduced a more advanced AI model that greatly improved image sharpness and artifact reduction. DLSS 3, featured in the RTX 40-series, takes things further by integrating Frame Generation, where AI predicts and inserts entire frames between rendered ones, effectively doubling the frame rate in supported games.

From single-player story-driven adventures like Cyberpunk 2077 to fast-paced shooters like Call of Duty: Warzone, DLSS has revolutionized how games are optimized for modern hardware.

How AI Upscaling Improves Resolution and Frame Rates

Traditional resolution scaling methods rely on brute-force rendering, meaning that a game must process every pixel on the screen in real time. The higher the resolution, the more computational power is required. For example, rendering a game at 4K resolution (3840x2160) requires four times the pixels of 1080p, putting immense strain on even the most powerful GPUs.

DLSS changes this dynamic by rendering the game at a lower resolution (e.g., 1440p) and then upscaling it to 4K using AI-trained models. Instead of relying solely on GPU processing power, DLSS leverages NVIDIA's Tensor Cores—specialized AI processors built into RTX GPUs—to intelligently reconstruct details, improving clarity and sharpness.

One of the biggest advantages of AI upscaling is its ability to predict missing details. Rather than merely stretching an image, DLSS analyzes previous and current frames, compares patterns, and reconstructs fine details that would typically be lost in standard upscaling techniques. This results in an upscaled image that closely resembles a native-resolution render, with minimal performance loss.

The Benefits of AI Upscaling

Lower internal resolution

hardware, including older GPUs and consoles.

3. Price vs. Performance:

NVIDIA's high-end RTX GPUs are often more expensive but deliver top-tier ray-tracing performance.

AMD's GPUs provide competitive ray-tracing capabilities at more affordable prices, making them attractive for budget-conscious gamers.

4. Game Optimization:

Some games are optimized specifically for NVIDIA RTX or AMD Radeon, so performance can vary depending on the title. Checking benchmarks for your favorite games can help inform your GPU choice.

Chapter 6

Textures, Shaders, and Rendering Techniques

The realism of modern video games is a result of intricate visual details that bring virtual worlds to life. From the rough surface of a stone wall to the shimmering reflection on a water puddle, every element is carefully designed to enhance immersion. Textures, shaders, and rendering techniques play a crucial role in achieving these lifelike visuals, blending art and technology to create rich, interactive environments.

Textures define the surface appearance of objects, while shaders control how light interacts with them, determining properties like reflection, transparency, and shading.

Rendering techniques bring everything together, optimizing visual quality without overloading the hardware. Developers constantly refine these elements to achieve a balance between realism and performance, ensuring that games look stunning while running smoothly.

As gaming technology advances, new approaches to textures, shaders, and rendering emerge, pushing the limits of graphical fidelity. From physically based rendering (PBR) to real-time ray tracing, these advancements make virtual worlds more convincing than ever before.

What Are Textures and How Are They Applied?

Textures are one of the fundamental building blocks of 3D graphics. In simple terms, a texture is a 2D image that is wrapped around a 3D object to provide it with color, detail, and realism. Without textures, game worlds would appear flat and featureless, as 3D models by themselves are simply geometric wireframes.

The Texture Mapping Process

Applying textures to 3D models involves several steps:

1. Texture Creation

Artists design textures using software like Adobe Photoshop, Substance Painter, or procedural texture generators such as Quixel Mixer.

These images simulate real-world materials such as wood grain, brick patterns, rusted metal, or polished marble.

2. UV Mapping

A 3D model is "unwrapped" into a flat 2D plane, much like unfolding a cardboard box.

This UV map tells the game engine how the 2D texture should be wrapped around the 3D object.

3. Texture Resolution and Detail

Textures are measured in pixels (e.g., 1024x1024, 2048x2048, or even 8K).

Higher resolutions provide finer detail but require more GPU memory, leading developers to use techniques like mipmapping (reducing texture resolution for distant objects).

4. Multiple Texture Layers

Many objects use multiple texture types to add complexity:

Diffuse (Albedo) Texture – The base color and pattern of the object.

Normal Map – Simulates fine surface details without increasing polygon count.

Specular Map – Controls how shiny or reflective a surface is.

Roughness Map – Determines how light scatters across a surface.

5. Rendering the Final Image

The game engine combines textures with shaders, lighting, and physics calculations to produce the final scene.

Optimizing Textures for Performance

Because high-resolution textures can be memory-intensive, developers use optimization techniques such as:

Texture Compression – Reduces file size while maintaining detail.

Mipmapping – Stores multiple versions of a texture at different resolutions, automatically selecting the appropriate level of detail based on distance.

Level of Detail (LOD) – Uses lower-resolution textures on distant objects to save processing power.

Texture Streaming – Loads textures dynamically as needed, reducing memory usage in open-world games.

By carefully balancing texture resolution and performance optimization, developers can create visually stunning games that run efficiently even on limited hardware.

The Role of Shaders in Creating Dynamic Environments

While textures define the appearance of an object, shaders determine how light interacts with that object. Shaders are small programs that run on the GPU, controlling everything from surface reflections to atmospheric effects.

How Shaders Work

Shaders operate at different stages of the rendering pipeline:

1. Vertex Shaders – Affect the shape and position of 3D objects. These shaders can create effects like water ripples, waving grass, or morphing character models.

2. Pixel (Fragment) Shaders – Determine how each pixel on the screen is colored and shaded. These are responsible for lighting, reflections, transparency, and material properties.

3. Compute Shaders – Perform advanced calculations, often used for physics simulations, AI, or complex visual effects.

Types of Shaders in Game Development

Different shaders are used to create a variety of visual effects:

Lighting Shaders – Control how light interacts with surfaces, including soft shadows, reflections, and ambient lighting.

Water Shaders – Simulate realistic water with reflections, refractions, and dynamic waves.

Glass Shaders – Recreate transparent and refractive surfaces like windows and lenses.

Toon Shaders – Give games a cel-shaded, cartoon-like appearance, commonly used in stylized games.

Dissolve Shaders – Create effects where objects fade or burn away dynamically.

Realistic Shading Techniques

Modern games rely on advanced shading models to achieve realism:

Physically Based Rendering (PBR) – Uses real-world material properties to simulate how light reacts with surfaces.

Subsurface Scattering – Allows light to penetrate materials like skin, making characters look more lifelike.

Ray-Traced Shading – Uses real-time ray tracing to calculate precise reflections and shadows.

Shaders bring game worlds to life, creating atmospheric depth, realism, and artistic style. However, because shaders require significant computational power, developers optimize them using caching, precomputed lighting, and shader LOD techniques.

Normal Maps, Bump Maps, and Specular Maps – Adding Depth and Realism

While textures provide base colors and patterns, additional maps help create depth, highlights, and surface details without increasing polygon count.

Normal Maps vs. Bump Maps

Bump Maps – A grayscale texture that simulates small surface details by manipulating shading. However, it doesn't actually affect the geometry.

Normal Maps – A more advanced version of bump mapping, using RGB color channels to create directional lighting effects, making surfaces appear 3D without adding extra polygons.

Specular and Roughness Maps

Specular Maps – Determine how shiny or reflective a surface is. For example, metal surfaces have high specularity, while wood has low specularity.

Roughness Maps – Work with PBR shaders to define how much light scatters across a material's surface.

These mapping techniques allow developers to create detailed, realistic environments without overwhelming the game engine.

How Developers Optimize Textures for Performance

High-quality graphics can strain even the most powerful GPUs, which is why developers use several techniques to optimize textures and shaders for better performance.

1. Texture Streaming

Instead of loading all textures at once, the engine loads only those that are currently visible. This is critical for open-world games like Red Dead Redemption 2 and Cyberpunk 2077, where thousands of textures are used.

2. Mipmapping

Lower-resolution versions of textures are used for distant objects, reducing GPU workload without affecting visual quality.

3. Level of Detail (LOD) Scaling

The game dynamically swaps out high-resolution textures for lower ones as objects move farther from the player's view.

4. Shader Optimization

Developers tweak shaders to minimize unnecessary calculations, using techniques like precomputed lighting, occlusion culling, and texture atlases to reduce GPU strain.

By balancing visual fidelity and performance, developers ensure that games look stunning and run smoothly, even on a range of hardware configurations.

Chapter 7

Shadows, Reflections, and Lighting Effects

Lighting is one of the most important aspects of video game graphics, shaping everything from the mood of a scene to the realism of its environments. Properly implemented lighting makes game worlds feel immersive, enhancing depth, atmosphere, and visual storytelling. Whether it's the warm glow of a sunset casting long shadows across a cityscape or the eerie flickering of a torch in a dark dungeon, lighting plays a critical role in how players experience a game.

Shadows and reflections further enhance this realism, providing the depth and interaction necessary to make environments feel dynamic. In the past, lighting effects were often faked using static techniques, but advancements in real-time rendering and ray tracing have brought game lighting closer to real-world physics than ever before.

However, achieving realistic lighting comes with a cost. Rendering realistic shadows, reflections, and global illumination in real time requires enormous computational power. Developers must carefully balance realism and performance, using various lighting techniques and optimizations to ensure smooth gameplay while maintaining high-quality visuals.

How Lighting Impacts Realism in Games

Lighting determines how objects, environments, and characters are perceived in a game. The way light interacts with surfaces influences realism, affecting brightness, shadows, reflections, and depth.

The Psychological Impact of Lighting

Beyond visual realism, lighting also affects game atmosphere and player emotions:

Warm lighting (golden sunsets, candlelight, fire) creates a sense of comfort, nostalgia, and intimacy. Many narrative-driven games use warm lighting to evoke emotions tied to safety and relaxation. Titles like The Legend of Zelda: Breath of the Wild employ golden-hour lighting to create breathtaking, serene landscapes.

Cool lighting (moonlight, neon glows, fluorescent bulbs) often conveys mystery, unease, or futuristic aesthetics. Games like Cyberpunk 2077 use neon-lit streets to enhance the cyberpunk atmosphere, while horror games rely on cold lighting to heighten tension.

Dynamic lighting (flashing lights, shifting shadows, dramatic spotlights) plays a significant role in immersion and gameplay. Horror games like Resident Evil 2 Remake utilize flickering bulbs and sudden changes in brightness to evoke fear and unease, while action-packed shooters use dynamic lighting to highlight key combat moments.

Beyond emotions, lighting also affects gameplay mechanics. Many stealth-based games incorporate light and shadow as functional elements, forcing players to avoid illuminated areas to remain undetected. Games like Splinter Cell and Dishonored use lighting as an interactive tool, allowing players to manipulate shadows for tactical advantage. Meanwhile, titles like Alan Wake turn light into a gameplay mechanic itself, with enemies being vulnerable only when exposed to bright light sources.

Lighting also affects player focus and guidance. Brightly lit areas often indicate points of interest, while darker areas can signal danger or hidden elements. Developers strategically use lighting to subtly guide players through levels, drawing attention to important objects, pathways, or interactions without the need for intrusive HUD markers.

The Science Behind Realism in Game Lighting

Game engines simulate light in different ways, but real-time rendering is always a challenge. In the real world, light behaves naturally, bouncing off surfaces and illuminating surroundings in a complex way.

Recreating this effect digitally requires sophisticated rendering techniques, including global illumination, ambient occlusion, and shadow mapping. These methods allow developers to simulate realistic lighting conditions while balancing performance constraints.

Techniques: Global Illumination, Ambient Occlusion, and Shadow Mapping

1. Global Illumination (GI) – Creating Natural Light Interactions

Global Illumination (GI) is a key factor in achieving realistic lighting in modern games. It simulates how light bounces off surfaces, filling areas with indirect lighting rather than relying solely on direct light sources. Without GI, scenes can look overly harsh or artificial, as objects are either too bright or too dark with little light diffusion.

Types of Global Illumination:

Precomputed GI – Used in older or performance-focused games, this technique calculates light interactions before gameplay begins, saving processing power. It works well for static environments but lacks flexibility for dynamic lighting.

Real-time GI – Actively recalculates how light interacts with surfaces, making it ideal for dynamic scenes but more demanding on hardware.

Ray-Traced GI – The most advanced form, using ray tracing technology to simulate realistic light bounces, but requires high-end GPUs like NVIDIA RTX or AMD Radeon RX 7000 series.

Titles like Cyberpunk 2077 and Metro Exodus utilize real-time ray-traced GI, dramatically improving realism, depth, and light diffusion, but requiring AI-driven upscaling (DLSS, FSR) to maintain performance.

2. Ambient Occlusion (AO) – Adding Depth to Shadows

Ambient Occlusion (AO) enhances realism by darkening areas where light has difficulty reaching, such as corners, crevices, and intersections between objects. This prevents game environments from looking flat and artificial.

Common Ambient Occlusion Techniques:

Screen Space Ambient Occlusion (SSAO) – A fast, widely used technique that estimates shading based on the depth of nearby objects.

Horizon-Based Ambient Occlusion (HBAO) – An improved version of SSAO, producing smoother, more realistic shadowing.

Ray-Traced Ambient Occlusion (RTAO) – The most advanced approach, using ray tracing to simulate accurate indirect shadows in real-time, but at a higher computational cost.

AO ensures that objects feel grounded in the environment, reducing the "floating object" effect seen in older games.

3. Shadow Mapping – Bringing Realistic Shadows to Life

Shadows enhance depth perception and create a stronger sense of realism. Without them, characters and objects feel disconnected from the game world. However, generating accurate, dynamic shadows is one of the most demanding graphical processes.

Types of Shadow Techniques:

Shadow Maps – A widely used technique that renders a scene from a light source's perspective, creating a depth map that determines which areas should be shadowed.

Soft Shadows – Simulates natural penumbra (soft shadow edges), preventing harsh, unnatural shadow lines.

Cascaded Shadow Maps (CSM) – Used in open-world games, allowing shadows to remain sharp up close while fading smoothly into the distance.

Ray-Traced Shadows – The gold standard, offering physically accurate shadow casting, but requiring dedicated ray-tracing hardware.

Games like Control and Cyberpunk 2077 use ray-traced shadows to create hyper-realistic lighting effects, eliminating common issues like shadow pop-in and unrealistic hard edges.

Real-Time Reflections vs. Pre-Baked Reflections

Reflections are crucial for immersive graphics, ensuring that mirrors, windows, water, and metal surfaces react realistically to light. However, rendering real-time reflections in video games is incredibly resource-intensive.

Pre-Baked Reflection Techniques (Static but Efficient)

Cubemaps – A pre-rendered 360° image applied to reflective surfaces. This method is cheap and efficient but cannot reflect moving objects dynamically.

SSR (Screen Space Reflections) – Uses on-screen data to approximate reflections. It works well for wet surfaces and glossy floors, but breaks down when objects move out of view.

Real-Time Reflection Techniques (Dynamic but Demanding)

Planar Reflections – Used for flat reflective surfaces like mirrors and calm water. Requires extra rendering passes, increasing GPU load.

Ray-Traced Reflections – The most advanced technique, accurately simulating complex reflections and transparency effects, but demanding high-end GPUs for real-time performance.

Games like Battlefield V and Cyberpunk 2077 utilize ray-traced reflections for stunningly realistic water, metal, and glass reflections, significantly enhancing immersion.

Balancing Performance and Realism in Lighting Design

Lighting effects are among the most hardware-intensive aspects of modern game rendering. Developers must optimize these systems carefully to maintain playable frame rates while still delivering visually stunning experiences.

1. Hybrid Lighting Approaches

Many modern games combine pre-baked and real-time lighting for efficiency:

Static environments use precomputed lighting to reduce computational load.

Dynamic objects, characters, and interactive elements use real-time lighting for accuracy.

This hybrid technique balances performance and realism, ensuring smooth gameplay without sacrificing quality.

2. Level of Detail (LOD) Adjustments

Lowering shadow and reflection quality for distant objects reduces GPU workload.

Disabling high-cost lighting effects when off-screen helps preserve performance.

3. AI-Driven Upscaling (DLSS, FSR, XeSS)

Using AI-powered resolution scaling techniques allows games to render lighting effects at lower resolutions while upscaling them intelligently, reducing performance impact while maintaining visual clarity.

Titles like Cyberpunk 2077 and Dying Light 2 leverage DLSS and FSR to enable ray-traced lighting at playable frame rates.

Chapter 8

Frame Rates, Resolution, and Performance Optimization

Smooth gameplay and sharp visuals are the cornerstones of a great gaming experience. However, achieving both simultaneously requires careful optimization. Frame rates, resolution, and various graphical technologies play a crucial role in determining how fluid and visually stunning a game looks. Whether it's the silky-smooth motion of a 120 FPS shooter or the crisp details of a 4K open-world adventure, balancing performance and graphics is a constant challenge for developers.

In this chapter, we'll explore frame rates (FPS), resolution, screen synchronization technologies like V-Sync and G-Sync, and the methods developers use to optimize performance without compromising visual quality.

Understanding FPS (Frames Per Second) and Why It Matters

Frame rate, measured in frames per second (FPS), determines how many images (frames) are displayed per second. A higher FPS results in smoother, more responsive gameplay, while a lower FPS can make motion appear sluggish and unresponsive.

Common Frame Rate Targets:

30 FPS – Often seen in console games, considered playable but not ideal for fast-paced action.

60 FPS – The standard for PC gaming and high-performance console games, offering smooth and responsive gameplay.

120 FPS & 144 FPS – Preferred in competitive gaming for ultra-smooth performance.

240 FPS & Above – Used by esports professionals with high-refresh-rate monitors for the most responsive experience.

Why FPS Matters:

Responsiveness – Higher frame rates reduce input lag, making controls feel more precise.

Visual Smoothness – Motion appears more fluid, particularly in fast-paced games like shooters and racing titles.

Reduced Motion Blur – High FPS minimizes blur and ghosting, enhancing clarity in motion-heavy scenes.

However, achieving high FPS requires powerful hardware and optimization techniques to ensure stable performance.

1080p vs. 4K vs. 8K: How Resolution Affects Visuals

Resolution refers to the number of pixels displayed on the screen, affecting image clarity and detail.

Common Resolutions in Gaming:

720p (HD, 1280x720) – Used in older or low-power devices.

1080p (Full HD, 1920x1080) – The most common gaming resolution, balancing clarity and performance.

1440p (2K, 2560x1440) – A popular choice among PC gamers, offering better visuals without the extreme demands of 4K.

4K (Ultra HD, 3840x2160) – Provides incredible detail, but requires powerful GPUs for high FPS.

8K (7680x4320) – The highest mainstream resolution, but impractical for gaming due to extreme hardware demands.

How Resolution Impacts Performance:

Higher resolutions require more GPU power to render detailed images, which can lower FPS. For example:

1080p at 120 FPS requires significantly less processing power than 4K at 60 FPS.

Many developers use dynamic resolution scaling (DRS) to adjust resolution on the fly, maintaining stable performance.

To balance resolution and FPS, many gamers use DLSS (Deep Learning Super Sampling), FSR (FidelityFX Super Resolution), or XeSS (Intel's AI upscaling) to boost frame rates while maintaining high image quality.

V-Sync, G-Sync, and FreeSync – Preventing Screen Tearing

Screen tearing occurs when the frame rate and monitor refresh rate are out of sync, causing visible horizontal splits in the image. To prevent this, various synchronization technologies are used.

1. V-Sync (Vertical Synchronization)

Forces the GPU to match the monitor's refresh rate, preventing screen tearing.

Cons: Can introduce input lag and lower FPS when frames don't align perfectly.

2. G-Sync (NVIDIA) & FreeSync (AMD)

Adaptive sync technologies that adjust the monitor's refresh rate to match the FPS output of the GPU.

Pros: Eliminates tearing without input lag.

Cons: Requires a compatible monitor and GPU (G-Sync for NVIDIA, FreeSync for AMD).

3. VRR (Variable Refresh Rate) on Consoles

Modern consoles like PlayStation 5 and Xbox Series X support VRR, dynamically adjusting the refresh rate for smoother visuals.

By using adaptive sync technologies, developers and gamers can eliminate visual artifacts while maintaining smooth gameplay.

How Game Developers Balance Graphics and Performance

Achieving the perfect mix of high-quality visuals and smooth performance is one of the biggest challenges in game development. Developers use various optimization techniques to ensure stable FPS without sacrificing graphical fidelity.

1. Level of Detail (LOD) Scaling

Reduces the quality of distant objects to save processing power.

Games like The Witcher 3 and Horizon Zero Dawn use LOD scaling to maintain high FPS without affecting nearby details.

2. Dynamic Resolution Scaling (DRS)

Adjusts resolution in real time to prevent FPS drops.

Seen in games like God of War (2018) and Halo Infinite, where resolution lowers temporarily in action-heavy scenes.

3. AI-Powered Upscaling (DLSS, FSR, XeSS)

Uses machine learning to render at lower resolutions while upscaling the image for a sharp final output.

NVIDIA's DLSS, AMD's FSR, and Intel's XeSS allow high-resolution gaming with less performance loss.

4. Culling & Occlusion Techniques

Prevents rendering objects that the player can't see (behind walls, off-screen, etc.).

Saves GPU resources, boosting FPS without affecting visible areas.

5. Ray Tracing Optimization

Ray tracing creates realistic lighting but is extremely demanding.

Developers use hybrid ray tracing, combining pre-baked lighting with real-time reflections to balance performance.

Games like Cyberpunk 2077 and Control offer ray-tracing modes with DLSS to achieve playable frame rates.

6. Shader Optimization & Texture Streaming

High-quality textures are loaded only when needed, reducing memory usage.

Many open-world games stream assets dynamically to prevent long load times.

7. Frame Rate Capping & Performance Modes

Many modern games offer performance modes (60+ FPS) and quality modes (higher resolution, lower FPS).

Players can choose based on their preference: smoother gameplay vs. better visuals.

Conclusion

The evolution of gaming graphics has been nothing short of extraordinary. From the pixelated sprites of early arcade games to the hyper-realistic visuals powered by real-time ray tracing and AI-driven upscaling, video games have continuously pushed technological boundaries. What was once a medium defined by simple 2D visuals has now transformed into an immersive experience that mirrors reality, offering players breathtaking environments, lifelike characters, and cinematic storytelling.

At the heart of this evolution lies a fundamental challenge: the balance between realism and performance. High-fidelity visuals demand significant computational power, and game developers must constantly optimize their techniques to ensure smooth performance across a wide range of hardware. From the introduction of textures and shaders to the advancements in lighting techniques, resolution scaling, and frame rate optimization, every step in gaming's graphical evolution has been driven by the need to achieve visual realism without compromising playability.

As we look to the future, emerging technologies like AI-powered image enhancement, real-time ray tracing, and machine learning-driven rendering are set to redefine gaming yet again. The current state of game graphics is already impressive, but breakthroughs in hardware and software continue to push the limits of what is possible. The pursuit of photorealistic visuals has led to remarkable advancements in rendering techniques, allowing developers to create worlds that feel increasingly real. The evolution of graphics has been a journey from simple pixel-based visuals to fully realized 3D environments, with each generation of gaming hardware enabling more sophisticated effects and greater levels of detail.

Video game graphics have come a long way since the early days of gaming. The first video games featured rudimentary visuals, relying on simple shapes and colors to represent objects and characters. Games like Pong and Space Invaders used basic pixel art and limited animation, yet they laid the foundation for what was to come. As technology advanced, sprite-based graphics in the 8-bit and 16-bit eras introduced more detailed characters and environments. Games like Super Mario Bros. and The Legend of Zelda demonstrated how visuals could enhance storytelling and gameplay. The jump to 3D rendering in the late 1990s with titles like Quake, Final Fantasy VII, and Tomb Raider marked a major turning point, allowing for fully explorable worlds and more complex character models.

With the arrival of modern game engines such as Unreal Engine and Unity, developers gained access to powerful rendering tools, enabling them to create lifelike textures, dynamic lighting, and sophisticated animation systems. The introduction of real-time physics, particle effects, and high-resolution textures pushed graphics to new heights, making virtual worlds feel increasingly immersive. The latest breakthroughs in ray tracing, AI-powered upscaling, and advanced rendering techniques are now bringing gaming closer to photorealism than ever before. Games like Cyberpunk 2077, Red Dead Redemption 2, and Horizon Forbidden West showcase how high-quality textures, realistic lighting, and dynamic environments can create worlds that feel alive. However, achieving this level of visual fidelity comes with a significant computational cost.

One of the greatest challenges in game development is finding the right balance between graphical realism and performance optimization. While high-resolution textures, ray-traced reflections, and advanced shading techniques can make a game look stunning, they also require significant processing power. This can lead to performance issues such as low frame rates, screen tearing, and input lag, particularly on lower-end hardware. Developers must employ various optimization strategies to ensure that games run smoothly while maintaining visual fidelity. AI-powered upscaling technologies like NVIDIA DLSS and AMD FSR have revolutionized performance optimization, allowing games to run at higher frame rates while retaining sharp, detailed visuals. Variable rate shading, dynamic resolution scaling, and advanced level-of-detail systems further improve efficiency, ensuring that rendering resources are allocated where they matter most.

Artificial intelligence is playing an increasingly important role in the evolution of video game graphics. AI-driven techniques like deep learning, procedural generation, and intelligent image processing are helping developers create more realistic environments, lifelike animations, and efficient rendering pipelines. One of the most significant AI-driven advancements is Deep Learning Super Sampling (DLSS). This technology uses neural networks to intelligently upscale lower-resolution images, allowing games to achieve higher frame rates without sacrificing visual quality. The result is a near-native 4K experience that requires far less GPU power than traditional rendering methods.

Similarly, procedural generation powered by AI enables the creation of massive, detailed game worlds with minimal manual input. Games like No Man's Sky and Microsoft Flight Simulator use AI-driven algorithms to generate landscapes, weather patterns, and ecosystems, creating environments that feel vast and organic. AI is also revolutionizing character animation. Machine learning-driven animation systems allow for more natural movements and realistic physics interactions. Rather than relying on pre-set animations, AI can dynamically generate character actions based on context, making NPCs and enemies feel more responsive and lifelike. As AI technology continues to advance, we can expect even greater improvements in real-time rendering, physics simulation, and environmental interactions, pushing video game graphics closer to photorealism than ever before.

Ray tracing has been one of the most groundbreaking developments in video game graphics. Unlike traditional lighting techniques that rely on approximations, ray tracing simulates the actual behavior of light, creating more realistic shadows, reflections, and global illumination. With the release of hardware-accelerated ray tracing GPUs, games can now feature dynamic lighting that reacts realistically to the environment, enhancing immersion and visual fidelity. Titles like Control, Cyberpunk 2077, and Minecraft RTX showcase how ray tracing transforms game worlds, adding depth, realism, and cinematic-quality lighting. However, real-time ray tracing remains computationally demanding, requiring significant hardware power to run smoothly. Developers are addressing this challenge by combining ray tracing with traditional rendering techniques, ensuring that games can achieve a balance between visual quality and performance.

Looking forward, the future of gaming graphics is set to be even more advanced, immersive, and efficient. As GPUs become more powerful and rendering techniques improve, real-time photorealism will become the standard for AAA games. AI-generated content will continue to revolutionize game development, from procedural world generation to intelligent animation systems that adapt to player behavior. Fully ray-traced worlds may become the norm, eliminating traditional rasterization in favor of more accurate, physically based rendering. Cloud-based gaming services will further democratize high-end graphics, allowing players to experience cutting-edge visuals on lower-end devices through real-time streaming. Virtual and augmented reality will also benefit from advancements in rendering technology, making immersive experiences more realistic and interactive than ever before.

The gaming industry has always been at the forefront of technological innovation, constantly redefining what is possible with each new generation of hardware and software advancements. The journey from 2D sprites to real-time ray tracing, AI-driven upscaling, and fully immersive environments has been nothing short of remarkable. Each breakthrough has brought gaming closer to the ultimate goal of creating worlds that are indistinguishable from reality. The continued progress of gaming graphics is boundless, and as technology advances, players can look forward to even more breathtaking, immersive, and dynamic experiences. The future of gaming is brighter than ever, and the relentless pursuit of graphical excellence ensures that the industry will continue to push the limits of what is possible, offering players extraordinary visual experiences for years to come.